Life

and Other

Natural

Disasters

Life
and Other
Natural
Disasters

David Russell
Bordowitz

LetterToTheWorld.com

ISBN 978-0-9733758-2-4

This book is dedicated to me.
Thanks.

table of wisdom

introduction

Allow me to introduce yourself. You are now in possession of a new breed of self-help book unlike anything ever before conceived. A survival guide, if you will, providing in-depth analysis and expertise on the various perils and tribulations of existence on this planet, and whatever other miscellaneous minutiae I deem appropriate to expound upon that I think may enlighten you.

Where most self-help books endeavour to help in a specific area, this one does not—rather, it allows the reader to take in all the information provided in each chapter and decide how best to apply it to help themselves. It's sort of like one of those "choose your own adventure" books, except there aren't really any other choices, and there's no adventure. Having no predefined boundaries or purpose ensures the reader walks away feeling satisfied with the book however they choose to perceive it while at the same time validating all the time I wasted writing it.

As for me, my name is David, known affectionately in academic circles as Chernobyl. This nickname was no doubt derived from the fact that my head reminds people of an unstable nuclear reactor. Now before you start thinking I don't sound like somebody who should be giving advice, I simply ask you to consider that nuclear reactors generate a *lot* of power before making vast areas of land uninhabitable for generations, so I suggest you make the most of what I have to offer before my next meltdown. My unique outlook on the world is now a treasury from which you can draw upon to help you with the profound enigma that is life in general.

Perhaps you often find yourself asking: "What is this life all about? Why is all this happening to me? Why am I here?" Maybe you struggle with asking too many questions all the time and being extremely annoying. At least that's how it looks from where I'm sitting. I guess I've got my work cut out for me, so let's get started...

chapter 1:
life is difficult

L et's cut right to the chase: life is extremely difficult. Hardships befall us on a daily basis, people die, and most dreams never come true, especially yours, so you might want to spend a few extra minutes in front of the mirror each morning practicing your best crying face. You're going to be using it a lot in the years to come.

God, in all His infinite wisdom and glory, has made all kinds of spectacular natural disasters which occur around the globe at His leisure, but nothing compares to the wondrous and magnificent disaster that is the free will that He bestowed upon us. As stupendous as the greatest earthquakes and tornadoes and other disasters must be to watch from on high (some of which we'll discuss in later chapters), one can only imagine the great awe with which He watches you and I, as we stumble through life making one monumental blunder after another with far-reaching consequences, creating a dust cloud larger than any asteroid strike ever could that looms over us, blotting out the sunlight and all hope like a nuclear winter from whence there is no escape.

In light of this, it is important to remember that our attitude during times of trial is what will determine the final outcome and the legacy we leave. Do you want to be the kind of person who cries out like a helpless victim being dragged down the street for miles behind the speeding bus of life with hair that looks like an abandoned bird's nest before rolling off the end of the highway and being left for dead in a ditch? Or do you want to be the roaring, fearless *lion*, who faces life with a terrifying scowl and legendary strength, before being shot by poachers and made into a throw rug that other people step on? The choice is yours.

It's easy to turn all the lights off and lay in the dark in the fetal position, listening to depressing music rather than face the daunting, daily responsibilities of human life. In fact, that's what I feel like doing right now rather than finishing this book and I'm only on the first chapter. But I can't be that selfish because I have a job to do and people obviously need my help. Well, maybe I'll just take a few hours. Be right back.

Okay I'm back. Now let's examine what the proper attitude should be then when faced with one of life's many, many, disasters. This will be good practice for you since one is likely right around the corner. It has been said that the only thing we can control for certain in life is our thoughts, so this is the one thing we must learn to use to our advantage when faced with difficulty, even though my first thought was that whoever said that had no idea what they were talking about.

Receiving bad news presents you with the opportunity to think about it in a way that is positive, and react accordingly. If something breaks, think of it as something you can fix. If it hurts, pretend you enjoy it. All the pretend games we play as a child can be seen as preparation for masks we must wear in the torturous adult life that is to follow. I can't tell you how many times I successfully pretended to enjoy various social functions when, in reality, licking a red-hot stove element would have been the more preferable experience. Maybe you can't really fix it. Maybe you can't really enjoy it. Maybe it's all going to blow up in your face. I can't remember where I was going with that train of thought so let's move on.

Something else we need to consider in preparation for life's difficulties is the surroundings with which we... surround ourselves. The environment in which we live and work has a profound influence on the attitude we have while facing unending horror and insurmountable odds every day. A cluttered house or office breeds cluttered thoughts and clumsy actions which frankly you cannot afford. The last thing we need while trudging through life is to navigate the added hazards of misplaced objects and slip and fall and dislocate our jaw so that we have to eat through a tube while dealing with everything else on our plate. Messy and disorganized bedrooms are a breeding ground for bad attitudes and a terrible way to wake up and start the day.

There are a number of reasons why your home might be a complete sty. Maybe your housekeeper is depressed too. You might think that since keeping your home clean is their job that you are not responsible, but it is actually a reflection of your bad leadership skills.

Motivating others and being a good leader are stepping stones to turning your life around and living one that is not centered on your own problems, but centered on helping other people fix them. In this case, there are several techniques at our disposal to use as motivation with respect to various household chores. For example, as a proud Canadian, I like to channel my inner curling champion whenever it is time to scrub the floor (Figure 1.1).

Figure 1.1 - Motivating your housekeeper

Yep!
Harrd!
HURRYYY!!
HURRY HARD!!

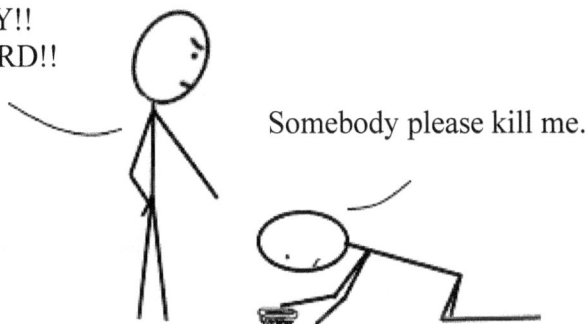

Somebody please kill me.

Having a clear and organized plan with a goal for your housekeeper will give them direction and something specific they can strive to achieve. In the above example, I have defined a clean floor as one in which I can see my own reflection. Though my floor is mostly carpet, it has nonetheless provided my housekeeper with a "long-term goal", which is an important requirement in living a fulfilling life. Now I have a clean house in which I can prepare to face life's difficulties, and have also enriched somebody else's life with purpose.

I'm sure by now it's becoming clear to you the kind of inspiration that awaits you in this book. I am just as excited as you are for this chance to share my experiences and the important lessons I've learned as I've meandered through the last three decades on the steady march towards old age and death that we're all on together. I'm sure you have lots of your own interesting anecdotes to share too, and that somebody out there cares to read them. See what I mean about pretending?

I think that's going to about cover it for today. I have a long list to prepare of all the areas of your life we need to address, and an even longer list of people to avoid, so let's meet back here tomorrow morning and pick up our examination of life on a lighter note that is more conducive to the brief feelings of hope that accompany the start of a new day. Obviously that will be a short chapter.

chapter 2: coffee

GOOD MORNING, SUNSHINE! I'm really sorry about yesterday. I know that my outlook can seem a little grim sometimes, but I promise that I have a much more exhilarating topic in mind for our one-way discussion this morning. It's about a powerful elixir that accomplishes the seemingly impossible task of giving us a reason to get out of bed in the morning, and it's called *coffee*.

I'm so excited about this topic that I can barely contain myself right now. I'll never forget the first time I ever had a coffee. I had intended to deliver the mysterious beverage to a friend at their place of employment (I am generally known for acts of charity of this magnitude), only to discover they were off that day. So there I was, driving back home with this "coffee" I had picked up at a drive-through, staring at it with a certain degree of curiosity and wonderment as it sat in the cup holder like a magic potion that had become undeliverable by some divine interference. Everyone I knew had to have their coffee in the morning and I never understood why.

"What is so special about this drink?" I asked myself. But there was no reply.

Rather than throw it out on the way into my building, I made the life-altering decision to bring it into my apartment and put it on the table.

I went about doing some various tasks, and every time I walked by the table, I saw the tall, brown take-out cup in the corner of my eye and heard an ominous whisper echoing throughout the room.

"Coffee-offee-offee-ee-ee-ee . . . Coffee-offee-ee-ee. . . chi-chi-chi-ah-ah-ah!"

After I scolded my housekeeper for hiding in the closet and whispering creepy things, there was still the whole issue of what to do with the coffee. Should I drink it? Should I dump it out?

"Maybe I'll just have a little taste," I thought, and brought the cup up to my lips.

"Hmmm... Well, it doesn't taste wonderful. I don't really get what the big deal is," I said to myself since nobody else was listening, and went back to what I was doing, which was probably nothing.

Suddenly a rush of energy seemed to come over my body as if I had just been injected with some kind of experimental drug. What a profound discovery!

"MAYBE THERE'S HOPE AFTER ALL!" I exclaimed in a voice that seemed to crack and shriek a bit as if I had just hit puberty.

I danced and whirled around my apartment, clasping the cup tightly in my hand with a smile on my face not unlike the one Jack Nicholson wore in *The Shining* when he first started to lose his marbles. This was my coffee! Mine! My own... Myyyyy *precioussss!!*

This was it! Life was going to be different now. I downed the rest of the drink quickly while simultaneously scribbling down mathematical equations on a pad of paper that were so complex I didn't understand them myself, but I think it had something to do with how to create an artificial black hole. Then I grabbed my housekeeper and twirled him so hard his apron flew up over his head.

"Dance with me!"

He ran out of the building screaming like Mrs. Dilber at the end of *A Christmas Carol* when Scrooge finally wishes her a Merry Christmas.

What should I do now? What should I do? WHAT SHOULD I DO? What should I dooooooo with all this newfound energy and enthusiasm for life?! Is there time to solve world hunger and cancer before the effects wear off? I pondered this and many other things while running laps around the dining table.

Hurriedly, I made arrangements to meet a friend at a coffee shop to have more coffee.

"I drink coffee now!" I yelled at her through my new perma-smile. Even though she was standing right in front of me, I knew that a louder and more forceful tone of voice would be necessary from now on. I needed to project! Like an actor delivering his lines to the furthest row in the theatre.

We sat at a table in a lovely cafe and drank lots of coffee and I engaged her in conversation with a passion and vigour hitherto unknown to me.

At one point our discussion spawned new ideas that excited my imagination so wildly I instinctively upstarted and kicked her in the face from across the table with such terrible force that for a moment her eyes appeared to be looking in different directions. We both laughed about it after. Everything was fun.

Then, a couple of hours later when I had returned home, my astonishingly good mood and strength of ten men seemed to vanish as quickly as it had been bestowed upon me. I became moody and lethargic. I hated everything. I hated my apartment. I hated life. And most of all, I hated you.

Over time I learned to control the adverse side effects that came when coffee's super powers left and returned me to a normal person, like a Planeteer who'd lost his ring. I came to accept it as part of life, and focussed on the knowledge that tomorrow morning I could have coffee once again, so long as I did not die in a horrible accident at some point during the day. Such a wonderful experience it was to finally have a reason to avoid those on purpose.

What an invigorating chapter! Let's move on.

chapter 3:
the importance of
solitude

In the unending struggle to maintain mental stability, it is important that we set aside some time once in a while for ourselves. This not only gives you time to collect your thoughts and reflect on the situations at hand with a clear head, but also gives the rest of us a much needed break from you as well.

To that end, I suggest a stroll through the forest, for it is only when we are surrounded by nature's beauty and distance ourselves from the comings and goings of civilization that we truly find our inner voice and make peace with the horrendous train derailment that is our daily lives. Few things in life will ever afford you the kind of care-free reverie that comes with wandering aimlessly through the forest with a red-breasted robin perched on your forefinger as you tilt your head to one side and belt out one of the Disney classics like "A Whole New World".

That being said, it is also extremely important to take certain precautions before venturing out into the wilderness, as the woodland presents certain dangers of its own, and to be ignorant of them is to invite serious injury or death. The many beasts that lurk in the wild are not to be taken lightly. You've probably heard the old adage many times that wild animals are "more scared of you than you are of them". Well I'm here to tell you there isn't a bear in the woods that wouldn't love to cross paths with you out there and smack you around for a while to blow off some steam. They have problems just like the rest of us. Maybe you thought it was the ideal life to do nothing most of the year except get as fat as possible so you can hibernate all winter but trust me, I've tried it and it's not all it's cracked up to be. They also never know when some yahoo with a rifle sitting in a tree might turn them into an accent piece or hang their hide on the wall as a trophy.

Which brings us to our next danger on our nature walk: *hunters*. I can't think of anything more irritating in life than getting deep into a good book surrounded by nature and the singing birds, only to end up with part of your face blown off by an over-zealous hunter who thought you were an indigenous animal, though some of you would hardly be in any position to blame them. If you thought just because you planned to spend the day in the forest that you didn't have to brush your hair, you may want to rethink that.

It is also a good idea to wear some brightly coloured clothing. Put a couple of fluorescent barrettes in your hair, or if you're planning to catch a few rays on the rock face, wear one of your neon braziers, though none of this will guarantee that you don't end up getting shot, especially if you're a man.

Never enter the forest without a compass. It is easier than you think to venture off the beaten path and end up lost in the wilderness with no sense of direction. If you've ever seen *Into The Wild*, you know you'll probably wind up spending your remaining days starving to death in an abandoned school bus, gagging on poisonous plant life. The only difference will be that you didn't end up there on purpose, but you'll be just as inept at finding sources of food. So, make sure to pack a lunch as well, but do not include any foods with a pungent aroma that will attract the wide variety of ferocious animals that can smell 3 to 5 miles away depending on wind and run the same distance faster than you can hide.

A sizable walking stick is also recommended, as many of the wild creatures carry rabies and you'll be glad to have something to fend them off with. Rabies is not a disease you want to find yourself catching, believe me. I've had many coworkers who were clearly carriers. They were constantly salivating, had a smart answer for everything and eventually had to be put down.

Now that we've covered all of the dangers of meditating in nature, it's time to practice your technique. Sit, cross your legs, hands down, palms up—be still. Recall the words of wisdom from all the great spiritual leaders who paved the way for us. Wasn't it the Dalai Lama who once said "If a tree falls in the forest and lands on somebody who was meditating, but there was nobody else to see it happen, can we really rule out homicide?" I'm guessing that was supposed to be rhetorical. Or was that an episode of *CSI*? I think the point is that being alone with nothing but our thoughts to keep us company allows us to examine such profound questions in greater depth without distraction, and also contemplate the very nature of our existence. Every sound is emphasized, every gust of wind felt with greater sensitivity, every sensation appreciated and enjoyed, experienced in full detail. Like when you drink too much and your favourite song comes on.

The goal should be to return to your coworkers, and return to your family and friends freed from all stress and frustration so that you have a clean slate for them to pile on all kinds of new stresses and frustrations. You'd be surprised how much crap you are capable of withstanding so long as it's new crap that varies, and all the people constantly slinging their crap at you have to change it up once in a while. You might also find a nice big steaming pile of crap in the forest to sling back at them when you come in the door. Those are the times you really know you've come back with a fresh new perspective and ready for new challenges.

chapter 4:
the magic properties
of candlelight

I'm sure we would all much rather be sailing, vacationing, or a number of other pastimes than facing the daily grind and an unending list of mundane chores that seem to make up the bulk of our futile existence. I know I'd rather be doing pretty much anything than writing this book right now. Sometimes it is not even the mounting pile of tasks that must be done, but an immovable form of hopelessness or depression that cannot be simply explained. So what can we do to make these times more enjoyable, or at least, more beautiful? Well, I'm glad I asked!

It may come as a surprise to you to learn there is a magic power in this world in the form of a manmade object, commonly known as the "candle", which can turn even the most monotonous daily chore into poetry in motion and a beauty to behold. If you don't believe me, I simply ask you to light a few candles and turn all the lights off the next time you have to do the dishes, and you will see an immediate difference in your attitude as you scrub those pots and pans. Where once you felt like the average poor soul buried in housework, you will now feel like the star of your own dramatic film, as the soft lighting flickers around you, casting your dancing shadow upon the wall, inspiring profound trains of thought and deep introspection. I ask you: what other magic in this world can make a person feel beautiful as they chisel away at a dried piece of pasta stuck to a plate?

And it doesn't end there. Candles have the power to make even the most humble home feel like a classic sanctuary in which passionate dreams are devised and achieved, and the person with very little feels they have all they need. Everything is all in the lighting. The proof is in a simple examination of world history as compared to the current day. People were more polite, thoughtful, creative, and better in general, and everything went downhill with the invention of the electric light bulb. I can't even imagine how much more productive a person I would have been had I been born long ago when everyone was forced to live out their evenings and nights with nothing but a few candles and the inspiration from their warm and subtle light. This book would have had a much different tone, that's for certain. Sure, I would have fallen down the stairs more often in lower lighting and burned my house down without any smoke detectors, but it would have been a small price to pay. Nowadays, the switch on every wall that offers bright and harsh artificial light is a temptation few are able to avoid for long.

Candles can also turn even the most horrible date gone awry into a romantic encounter with rich conversation. They can provide a setting so beautiful for your dinner guests that they don't notice your cooking is bad enough to kill a large horse. Moments of unbearable loneliness become an homage to the depth of your inner and outer beauty. There are evenings when I just stand in front of the mirror, basking in the ambient glow and marvel at my own reflection as a single tear rolls down my cheek and my housekeeper plays the violin in the background. Try that with a 100 watt bulb overhead making you look like a tired old hag and spotlighting each of your hideous flaws.

I don't feel like people put enough effort into making the most of simple tools like this to shine a new perspective onto their despair and make it tolerable and even beautiful. Maybe there is an epic poem inside you just waiting to come out, and all it will take is a tea light on the nightstand to bring it forth, and turn your misery into a source of inspiration for countless others. Just don't forget to blow it out before you fall asleep or you might roll over and set your blankets on fire and burn to death. Talk about poetic.

I wrote this chapter in candlelight. Need I say more?

chapter 5:
our health & fitness

The world is round indeed. Each year, millions of people make a new year's resolution to finally get in shape other than spherical, and fail miserably. If you've ever tried to go on a diet before, then you were already familiar with disasters long before you picked up this book. But our health does not only involve our physical bodies. Our mental health is just as important, if not more so. That's what I'm here for. I'll have you washing your clothes on your abs in no time and trimming some of that disgusting fat off your attitude while we're at it.

Let's start with the most common form of failure when it comes to improving our fitness: the *diet*. It's been scientifically proven that the reason almost all diets fail is because you lose weight off your brain first and forget you're supposed to be dieting. We quickly go from that plate of steamed vegetables for dinner each night to a hamburger or a pie-eating contest. Since we can't change the laws of physics, we're not even going to deal with dieting in this chapter. I'm afraid that will always be hopeless, not unlike most of your goals.

Then there's exercise. We all know that person who keeps buying the latest and largest piece of exercise equipment at great expense, like the Rowing Machine, or the Belly Buster, or the Butt Cracker, which ends up doing little more than collecting large quantities of dust in their house and showing the world how, not only can they not commit to their exercise plan, they're also embarrassingly behind in their housework. Maybe that person is you and now you're so insulted you've thrown this book out and promised yourself you'd never continue reading it again. Well we've already established you don't do what you say you're going to do, so I'm sure you'll fail at that too and be searching through the trash later to find out what else I have to say about you. Believe me, this is all for your own good. You'll be thanking me later. Or at least I will.

Now, since we've revealed that diets and exercise equipment are not the answer, you're wondering what else there is. The answer is *acrobatics*. Forget jogging, forget yoga, forget *Sweatin' To The Oldies*, acrobatics is where it's at.

Acrobatics is a form of physical disciplining that requires a limber and flexible body and a strict regime of rotating and inverted positions and stunt practices. The first thing you'll need to do so that you don't permanently hurt yourself is stretch out your muscles and improve your flexibility, especially in the leg and groin area. You may want to pick up a copy of my book *Learning To Do The Splits In Five Minutes* to get you started. It's a quick beginner's guide to getting your legs into the 180 degree angle required for many of the starter acrobatic moves using only two regular dining chairs and a high pain threshold. And if you like that book, I strongly suggest the international best-selling follow up: *Making The Most Of Your New Life In A Wheelchair*. Both books are readily available at your local bookstore, assuming you live in Uzbekistan.

I also suggest doing some research online to find out what some of the different moves are, as I do not have the required time to go into as much depth in this area as I probably should. It's far beyond the scope of this book anyway and besides that I'm already getting bored with this chapter. Try Google Images with the search term "acrobatics" to see some of the basics. You'll notice that a lot of the images show many group positions, and this is indeed something that can be a great deal of fun with a friend, so try to get them involved as well.

Another thing you can do to make the most of your skills as you acquire them is try to mix them into your daily life as frequently as possible for maximum benefit. For example, instead of walking to the store, try cartwheeling. You should see the kind of reaction I get from people passing by as I cartwheel down the sidewalk to the grocery store. I inspire far more awe and motivation with this simple exercise than the boring joggers who are trying to sweat off their cheeseburger. Anyone can jog. Even a pig can jog, but they can't cartwheel. Do you want to be a pig, or an acrobat? I'm guessing that question gave you far more pause than it probably should have.

Now that you're in physical shape, let's talk about your mental health. Some people are starving themselves in this area without realizing and don't really have much there that they can afford to lose. We have to keep feeding our minds healthy intellectual foods, metaphorically speaking, like books and films and art and spiritual works so that we feel our lives have purpose and meaning and we're progressing as human beings, but not feed them so much that we become mentally obese and completely space out when people are trying to talk to us because we're too busy over-complicating analogies with long-winded run-on sentences in our heads and analysing our intellectual stomach rolls that only show up when we bend over. I don't even know what that means, I just sort of ran with it. At least I've provided you with a perfect example of what happens when you become intellectually rotund. It's all about balance.

chapter 6: expert advice on air travel

Let's talk a bit about one of the world's most popular forms of transportation, as I know it is a source of anxiety and fear for many travellers who must use it to get from point A to B in a timely manner, and this chapter is for them. Literally thousands of passenger planes take off around the world every day, and if you've been following the news lately, you know that most of them crash long before reaching their destination.

Isaac Newton famously postulated that whatever goes up must eventually come down. What he failed to specify in this brilliant observation hundreds of years ago, is that it generally comes down a lot faster, and usually on fire. But as you've come to expect from previous chapters, I'm all about preparing people for the inevitable and helping them to make the most of any unpleasant situation.

I just have to get something off my chest first and I like to think I'm entitled since this is my book. I have a really hard time understanding the thought process of somebody who boards a plane, and I'm referring particularly to the small planes that are propelled by a single motor, knowing full well that if that motor should fail and stop for any reason, it will mean certain death.

Let's just say, for example, you could get the blade on your riding lawn mower rotating fast enough to lift you off the ground. Would you then use this as some ridiculous form of transportation? Commuting to work knowing that if that tired little motor stalled out, you would plunge to your death and a search party would be looking for your scattered remains throughout the forest and eventually find your hands clutched to the steering wheel of a lawn mower? Who chooses to die in this fashion? I can think of better ways.

And every time one of these planes drops out of the sky, there's a whole team of expert investigators searching the wreckage to find out what happened. I can tell you exactly what happened! They were basically flying a riding lawn mower that stalled! It's not some profound mystery!

Then there is all this intense importance placed on finding the "black box" so that the investigators can learn what the pilot was saying moments before the crash. I can save you a whole lot of time and effort and tell you what he was saying. It was probably something like "AAAAAHH!!!"

Anyway, all that aside, you've decided to use this method of travel for your next vacation, so let's talk about how to best prepare yourself for the likely event you're about to make headline news in all the wrong ways.

It is always best to arrive at the airport at least a couple of hours before your flight is scheduled to depart, due to all of the security checks in place to find the people who've made it their sole purpose in life to blow up the plane you're about to board.

Once you've made it through security, use your boarding pass to board the plane, find your seat, place your carry-on luggage in the overhead compartment, sit down and fasten your seatbelt, assume the crash position and remain that way for the duration of the flight.

The "crash position" is an airline safety measure in which you bend over and place your head between your legs. It evolved over many years from the ancient canine proverb: "There's no safer place for your head than your own crotch." The increased flexibility you acquired in the previous chapter will allow you to achieve this position with a little more dignity than the people around you, who will probably have to put their head between each other's legs.

This seating position also discourages small talk among passengers, which I recommend you avoid at all costs. If you've ever seen the movie *Alive*, you know you might wind up crashing somewhere in the Andes Mountains and having to survive by cannibalising your fellow passengers who were fortunate enough to be killed on impact. But hey, if you want to get all chummy with your future dinner, be my guest. It's also a good idea to pack salt and pepper shakers in your carry-on. Trust me, after surviving a traumatic, fiery descent, you're not going to feel like rummaging through the cargo hold looking for condiments, and I doubt that's a meal you want to have without seasoning.

Once you've crashed down in your new home which is likely thousands of miles away from civilization, it's time to start thinking about how you'll make a life for yourself here. That's assuming your flightpath didn't take you over the ocean, in which case you don't need to waste any time reading about survival.

Check the surrounding area for eatable plant life and shelter. Some of the techniques you learned in chapter 3 will be helpful to you here, except now you may have to deal with the eventual descent into madness of any other passengers who survived. Make sure to watch your back and look for any signs like trembling hands or paranoia. You'll have to take care of those people first, if you know what I mean.

Once you've set up a shelter and found alternate sources of food, you're going to have to put some effort into entertainment and deriving some form of joy out of whatever days you have remaining. For example, if you happened to crash down somewhere snow-covered, check the wreckage for any suitable piece that could be used as a toboggan and get out there on those hills. Try to laugh out loud often and really sell yourself on the idea of spending the rest of your life here. There is no point being miserable about circumstances we can't change. That is perhaps the most important lesson I will continue to drive home throughout this book.

chapter 7:
choosing the right
career path

It is my firm belief that most of us in this world were created with certain talents and abilities so as to equip us for performing a particular role or occupation that was meant for us. In this chapter, I shall endeavour to help you identify what exactly was meant for you, and how best to succeed at it. None of us want to see another actor who can't act, a pianist who can't pian, or a fire breather burn off their left eyebrow and part of their face in front of horrified spectators.

Identifying our God-given talents can be difficult, especially for those of you who don't have any. In such a case, you're going to have to be a bit more creative than most. We've already talked a lot about depression and hopelessness in past chapters, and if you don't feel like you're good at anything, we may have just found out what's causing the bulk of yours. This is what Oprah would call an "ah-ha moment". Those people might as well skip forward to the next chapter, since this one obviously won't apply to you.

The first step in identifying the right career choice for you is to examine what it is in life that you find most interesting. What do you feel drawn to? What brings you the most joy? I know right now you might be thinking it's time to start a grow op or whorehouse based on supply and demand and where the world is headed, but I'm going to suggest you think outside the box here and aim a little higher.

So now you're thinking: "Who are you to decide what's right or wrong for me? What if all I care about is drugs and sex?" Maybe you missed the part where you entered into a contractual author/reader arrangement that was spelled out in microscopic print for you on the back of the title page and which you agreed to by reading further, as set out in the Terms of Use. Though an electron microscope is required to view the agreement, section 89, subsection 12, paragraph 4 states that obtaining one is not my problem, and that by turning the page you accepted the terms and agreed to agree with me where required and as directed by the Author, including but not limited to any advice that pertains to agreeing with the agreement. That *is* why it's called an "agreement" after all. Who wastes time writing up a disagreement for people to disagree with? It's possible I missed my own calling as a lawyer, but I was compelled by a desire to write and help people ever since my first short story in high school. It was a tragedy about a student who threw himself out the window rather than have to finish the crappy writing assignments a cranky old English teacher kept forcing on him. It was a surprise hit among my fellow students, though not so much with the teacher.

Once you've established what it is you're interested in, it's important to choose an appropriate mentor whose work you admire and who can direct you in that particular field of study. If it's not obvious by now, I had chosen early on to model my life and career after the brilliant author and poet, Sylvia Plath.

For the few of you in the world who don't already know, Sylvia Plath was born in 1932 and grew up to become horribly depressed and emotionally tortured, in and out of mental hospitals, utilizing her profound and often dark brilliance to write some of the most beautiful works of poetry in history, until she eventually stuck her head in an oven and gassed herself to death. We could have been best friends. I've had to settle for the resulting "master and apprentice" relationship that has guided my writing career from beyond her grave. I like to think of myself as the Sylvia Plath of motivational and life improvement writers of my generation.

One point I really want to stress is that there are NO small or unimportant jobs. The collective workforce in what might be considered by some as lower tier occupations at burger joints and cafes are just as important, if not *more* important than those in privileged positions of power running the country, for without you, there is no country to run. I remind my housekeeper of this often while he is cleaning my toilet, and thank him daily for providing me a household to rule over.

chapter 8:
self-defence in
nightmares

Today, class, I'm going to teach you how to defend yourself against the creatures of the night who continually invade our dreams. You may have believed up until now that a "nightmare" was an occurrence over which you had no control, and you probably just lay there like a helpless victim, tossing and turning and sweating until you wake up screaming like some kind of pussy. Well, we're going to put a stop to that right now.

At some point in your life you've probably heard the advice from those so-called experts who are all "Never go to bed angry." Well I'm here to tell you that the exact opposite is the wiser course of action. In fact, you should always go to bed as pissed off as possible. That way, whenever someone tries to attack you in your dreams, you're already in the mood for a smackdown.

I will illustrate the correct way to handle the situation by using my own personal example from a couple of nights ago. The details of your nightmares may vary slightly, but the principles for self-defence against each villain remain the same.

We start off with how to react at the first encounter with your adversary. Now, in my nightmare, this was a big ugly axe murderer who longed for my untimely death. This particular nightmare was no doubt instigated by the vicious front desk clerk at The Woodsman Inn who yelled at me that evening for knocking a lamp over while cartwheeling through the lobby. We will call him Jack to simplify things.

When you come face-to-face with your adversary, the most important thing you must do is *stand your ground!* The killer/monster expects you to turn around and run for your life crying in fear like you always do, but you must not only stay put, but begin to make an angry face that is even angrier than theirs. It is a good idea to practice this before falling asleep each night. If you share your bed with a spouse, you can test it out on them first. Hold your gaze steady for no apparent reason and see if it scares or disturbs them. Don't tell them why or explain it to them or it will lose any effectiveness. If they end up losing sleep over it or refusing to turn their back on you during the night, you know that you've mastered the look. In your nightmare, this will no doubt instigate what we refer to as "the charge", not unlike waving a red flag in front of an angry bull. In my dream, this is when Jack began to run towards me, snarling, axe raised high.

One of the keys to winning in nightmares is to take advantage of the killer's weaknesses, and "the charge" may perhaps be the most exploitable of them all. I immediately went into preparations for the "crane kick", as previously made famous by *The Karate Kid*. By the time Jack ran the length of the creepy dark house to get to me, screaming like a banshee, I launched into one of the very most fiercest kicks to the face ever executed. I'm talking slow motion, badass Matrix style, striking him in the jaw with unbridled fury.

It is a pleasurable experience in life the first time you look down at your nightmare assailant, lying on the floor all pathetic-like with blood trickling from their mouth and a baffled look on their face as they try to figure out what went wrong. They're used to being the aggressor and in control, and losing that control makes them feel less scary and wonder about their future. After all, scaring people is all they've got in life. At this point, I reached down and grabbed Jack by the hair with one hand, and began to punch him repeatedly in the

51

face with the other, screaming wildly "Who's the scary one *now*, bitch?!"

He got up and ran out of the house, which brings us to step two: always pursue monsters and finish what you start. I know you're thinking that it might be a good window of opportunity to escape, but it is very important that we follow through. Chase that psycho down and make them rue the night they wandered into the wrong friggin' mind. I picked up the axe he dropped and pursued him into the forest as the fog rolled in. I recommend letting out a hearty laugh here as you give chase. Something like:

"HaaaaaaaaaaAAAAAAAAAHAHAHA-HAHAHAA-HAAAAAAAAAAAAAAHAHALALAHAHAZA!

AAAAAHAHAHAHAAAAAAAHSHSLAL;L;SDK;FJ;"

Once you achieve sufficient mental discipline, you may even be able to conjure up some background thunder and lightning for good measure.

With any luck, you'll wake up as I did just before committing the fatal blow. That way, he will survive to tell all his friends throughout the day, and your reputation will spread accordingly among nightmare villains. I'm sure you will find over time that your sleep is disturbed with less frequency, and you may even look forward to the next nightmare so you can kick a little ass. I've gotten so used to being the aggressor in my nightmares that monsters rarely even have the chance to come after me before I've already run straight for them and knocked a few of their teeth out.

Nightmares may vary widely among people who experience them, but the fundamentals are always the same. I hope this chapter will have given you the confidence you need to take charge of the experience. Don't stand outside the haunted house wondering and fearing what may be lurking inside. Get up there and kick that front door in and find the undead wench who lives there so you can educate her on what real fear is all about.

This concludes our lesson for today. Please be sure to practice and keep a journal of your progress, and maybe do something different with your hair tomorrow, because wow.

chapter 9:
sex

I'm sure my editor would love to take all the credit for the idea of including this chapter, and not just because I edited my own book. It is a common opinion that "sex sells", so I expect this chapter to afford me a very luxurious lifestyle going forward, and besides, what better topic for a book about natural disasters?

I'm going to venture a guess by the looks of you that you probably don't really know much about this topic and what it's all about, so I think we should start off with an explanation of this rather disgusting biological habit in a way that even the most inexperienced observer will be able to understand. I am all about catering to my audience. We can take a practical approach to better comprehending this animalistic behaviour by way of a little experiment which will demonstrate just exactly how sex works.

First, you're going to have to take a trip to your local pet store to pick up all the supplies we'll need to carry out this experiment:

1. One fish bowl.
2. Two fish. And not some kind of lame goldfish or whatever. I mean two of those "fighting fish" that you're not supposed to keep in the same tank together lest their barbaric instincts take over.

PROCEDURE:

1. Fill the fish bowl with water and set it on the table.
2. Place your two fighting fish into the bowl and observe how they begin to try and peck each other to death. This is what is commonly referred to as "foreplay".
3. Knock the bowl over, dumping the contents out onto the table.
4. Watch as the fish begin to flop around on top of each other, gasping for air until they finally lose consciousness and remain motionless and full of regret in their own wet, slimy, mess.

You now know everything there is to know about sex. This demonstration also clearly illustrates for us how sex ruins lives, as you will notice that both fish are now dead.

DISCLAIMER: This experiment is purely theoretical as I would never advocate harming any living creature other than a telemarketer. If you want to throw a couple of those in a tank and seal it up, by all means. You may think that has nothing to do with the topic at hand but just wait until you experience the resulting satisfaction. I need a cigarette just thinking about it.

Now that you know everything about what the act of sex entails, it's time to discuss how you can best avoid it in the future and not fall victim to the many misguided persons in the world who seek some kind of temporary endorphins by lowering themselves in this manner like a herd of wild sows during mating season.

As the world continually hurtles towards increasingly liberal views about sex, we must be even more vigilant nowadays than previous generations. People are far less reserved and much more blunt in their desire to engage in this practice. Figure 9.1 shows us one of the many forms in which a proposition for sex from a complete stranger may materialize while we are out and about, minding our own business:

Figure 9.1 - The proposition

Hey there!
I would like to get
naked and flop around
on you like a big fish!

K.

Person interested in sex   Victim

Though sex does have various applications, virtually all of them are evil in nature, such as propagation of the human race or the seducing of otherwise innocent and disciplined people. Maybe instead of being so concerned with climate control, wars, and excessive garbage overtaking the planet, we might think about how any twit with a libido can procreate and cause all of these problems in the first place. Don't get me wrong; if the majority of people could occupy the planet responsibly, I would be all for being fruitful and multiplying if that's your cup of tea, but sadly that is not the case.

People with issues related to insecurity also use sex as a way to bolster their ego by way of conquering another individual in this degrading fashion. There are much better ways to feel better about yourself than acting like a cave person. You might try meditation, or a shower, or self-help books. Just look at the wonders this one has already done for your self image and empowerment, and I've only just gotten started. Which makes me wonder why they're called "self-help" books, since I'm the one writing it and doing all the work and you're just sitting on your ass.

Anyway, I know from experience that no matter how much time I spend going over the dangers of sex, you will probably at some point in the future engage in it anyway despite my warning. Just don't come crying to me when you end up all diseased and pregnant. Especially if you're a man.

Personally, it's a level I have never lowered myself to, nor do I foresee myself making a monumental error in judgement like that in the years to come. Now then, onto Chapter 10: Lying.

chapter 10:
lying

"Oh, what a tangled web we weave
When first we practice to be a lyin' ass hoe."

Sir Walter Scott
[Translated into Modern English]

L et's talk a bit about a very common and distressing activity among humans that is even more classless than sex: lying. Our objective in this chapter will be not only to arm you with the skills necessary to detect those who practice this dark art, but also how to respond and protect yourself and your loved ones.

Lying is very much like singing in that, if you're not good at it, it's probably best to refrain to save the embarrassment of everyone involved. Unfortunately, it is commonplace for people to attempt this as a means of avoiding an undesirable circumstance or outcome, particularly with regard to their mistakes, even when they don't have the necessary skills or intelligence to pull it off.

In the olden days, one way that people dealt with compulsive liars was to cut their tongue out to prevent further falsehoods. While crude, this method was certainly effective and a tradition that I personally have tried to maintain in the modern era. One of my prized possessions is a pair of scissors with a belt holster that I acquired from a retired paramedic friend. These are not only a quick and convenient defence against those who would attempt to tell me an untruth and insult my intelligence, but also make for a very attractive fashion accessory, available in multiple colours and styles from your local emergency response supply store.

While it would be a romantic notion to call myself the lone soldier of truth who is fighting for justice in this way, I happen to be only one of a diverse group of people out there who maintain old fashioned values. In fact, whenever you encounter someone who seems to have nothing more than an innocent speech impediment, you may want to take whatever they're saying with a grain of salt, as one of us may have already tried to cut their tongue out.

Much like drug use and the prevalence of sexual exploitation, lying is one of the more common signs of moral decay that pervades modern society. Politicians, businessmen, lawyers, husbands, wives, Facebook users, all make frequent use of lying and contribute to the overall deceptive jungle that the rest of us must journey through. Lying has become so mainstream that most of us must actually assume whatever we're hearing is a lie until proven otherwise, turning friendships and relationships into a game of Stratego, where one must navigate a proverbial minefield of deception.

One of the easiest ways to detect a lie is to observe the facial expression of the person who is speaking. Look for any kind of twitching or inability to make eye contact while they're talking to you. Redness in the face, perspiration, and indigestion are all signs. That's why I've had a harder time knowing when people are lying about enjoying my cooking.

The trick is to keep the person talking until you can discern the truth, as liars tend to spin their web out of control the longer they go on. Use key Canadian responses to encourage them and show interest, like "yeah eh?" and "oh jeez". Eventually they'll lose track of what they said and tell two different versions of the same story in one sitting. I like to reach in and grab hold of their tongue at this point and stare them down as sort of a warning shot that I am not to be trifled with. This is usually sufficient to prevent further transgressions, and less messy. It is also mildly amusing if they try to keep talking.

If you're really feeling on top of your game that day, you may also make a stealthy attempt to hook them up to your portable lie detector. You can usually find a cheap one online but you might want to spend a little extra for one that you don't have to hook up to their nipples, as that can get a little more tricky depending on the nature of your relationship.

This is of course not the sort of moral high ground we should all seek to live on and not without its share of controversy either, so if I were you, I would try to stick to the old fashioned way of remaining truthful yourself, while reforming people by way of example. As the old saying goes: "An eye for an eye leaves everyone blind, but an eye for a tongue means you still have one eye left to see them keep trying to lie using sign language."

chapter 11:
the animal kingdom

If you're anything like me, you like animals a lot more than you like people, so I want to dedicate a chapter to our furry and adorable, unconditionally loving friends, even though some of the most beautiful ones in the wild would maul or gore us to death without hesitation if we got too close, and who could blame them? It's always been a risk I'm willing to take for that one big gratifying hug before facing the life beyond. Would you like to die alone of old age or in the arms of a big handsome polar bear? Not a tough choice in my book.

I believe animals represent the very finest of God's creations and serve to show humans what they could have been had they strived harder to achieve some level of unified virtue and grace. Animals have obviously provided mankind with a great deal of inspiration through the ages, pervading our art and literature, motivating us to try and fly like the birds in our clunky planes or traverse the deep like a dolphin in our ridiculous scuba gear and flippers. When you see bubbles emanating from a dolphin's mouth, they're laughing at you, just so you know, and being laughed at under water is basically the apex of humiliation. We have certainly failed to ever reach their natural ability to thrive and be one with our habitat. We're much better at blowing each other up and destroying the environment and things of that nature.

Our more domesticated animal friends are loyal and love without bias, will follow us wherever our hearts desire to go, providing a flawless kind of friendship through good times and bad that few humans can live up to. Granted that when it's time to take them to the vet they might freak out and pee all over the car, but I think we've all had human friends who behave even worse than that while trying to bring them to see a doctor. It is no wonder so many of us have chosen to live alone and in the company of only our beloved pets. My housekeeper just read this over my shoulder and insisted I recognize that he lives here too. Now you see what I mean about animals being far less annoying.

Recent and highly scientific studies have proven that people who spend time with animals sustain a higher and more consistent level of happiness than non-animal loving losers. I know that some of you nerds are looking for a footnote or "appendices" for details on the studies I refer to in this book and who conducted them and what not, so good luck with that. I don't subscribe to all those proper book formalities like other authors. Besides, I conducted them myself and the results were conclusive, so there's your footnote.

I have spent a great deal of time with a wide variety of species, monitoring my own increases in contentment as opposed to when I spend time with, oh I dunno, you for example. I am basically the next generation incarnation of Diane Fossey, except my research was all mainly indoors instead of the African jungle and more to do with puppies and cats than gorillas. Other than that, we're exactly the same. I also haven't been murdered yet, but the night is young.

I once spent an unfortunate amount of time at the zoo observing a gorilla regurgitate in his hands and eat it over and over again, so I'm not sure why her career studying that kind of behaviour is any more famous than mine. *Gorillas In The Mist* might have sold millions of copies and be considered the foremost book of its kind, but my book *Have Your Cake And Eat It Twice* was a lot more useful in my opinion. It never got the kind of attention from the scientific community that it warranted.

You can tell a lot about a person by their relationship with animals. The degree of compassion and love that is shown toward them generally translates into how much love and compassion they show other people. Those who are cruel to animals should never be trusted and/or should be locked away. Dogs are a good example of animals that are capable of sensing what kind of aura emanates from a person and will react to their presence accordingly. If I ever have a dog and he doesn't like you, there is no way you're coming into my house, and I hope you can run fast.

I adore all of those videos you can find online of people like Kevin Richardson who live among lions and tigers and play and cuddle with them with no fear of having their head bitten off. I had a cat that once enjoyed to be brushed only x number of strokes before it made him bitchy and he tried to bite me. I can only imagine what it must be like to piss off your pet lion. There must have been times those wild cat handlers tried to brush them on the wrong day and lost a limb. I can't say that it's a price I wouldn't be willing to pay for the opportunity.

Camels are another animal that I enjoy, and not just because they make good companions while traversing the desert. I like their big eyes and humps and how much they can drink in one sitting before long hauls when a refill might not be available. I have great respect for the way they've aided humanity throughout the ages, though I suppose that wasn't exactly by choice. It's safe to say, however, that if a camel ever chose to work for me, someone's job would be in jeopardy. I envision myself one day arriving at the Plaza Hotel with my camel carrying my luggage as I sing Drake's famous line "Started from the bottom now we're here." I'm just kidding of course. I would keep my housekeeper around because I'm sure my camel would need an assistant.

You've probably noticed that I limited this chapter to discussion about mammals only and not reptiles and amphibians etc. because they are gross. I always get along well with people who like animals but if you're one of those people who keeps a tarantula or giant snake as a pet then frankly you are probably kind of weird and we can't be friends. If I had a big snake in an aquarium I would imagine that every day when I got home from work, the first thing I would do is frantically check to see if it was still there, and if it ever wasn't, I would probably run screaming out into the street with my arms flailing and yelling "IT ESCAPED! RUN FOR YOUR LIVES!" And that's not what pet ownership is supposed to be about.

chapter 12:
insects shouldn't
exist

Insects are disgusting. They lurk in dark and dirty places, they bite, they're ugly, and should all die. I know what you're thinking: that all the beautiful creatures we discussed in the previous chapter that survive off them would die too, but I'm sure they would evolve to enjoy new and less gruesome sources of food. Besides, anything that would eat a bug is disgusting too. Before you go on about how beautiful birds are, consider that only moments before perching on the branch and singing so gay, it was probably crunching down on a cockroach or gagging on an earthworm. Yeah, how majestic. I'm not interested in all the biological technobabble about how the entire food chain would collapse and humanity would die out. If you want to argue those points, go write your own book. This one is mine and I have the floor right now.

If only God had told Noah to take two of everything on the arc except for insects. Imagine: two of every kind of creepy crawly thing. How would you like to have been a passenger on that cruise ship? I would have spent every night of that voyage curled up in a ball behind the pair of anteaters. Now there's an example of God's greatness. I feel like the anteater was God realizing he shouldn't have made insects so He designed an animal with a vacuum attached to its face to clean them up. Sadly, He didn't make enough of them. I keep one in my apartment at all times as a natural form of pest control. I named him Dyson.

I should probably have called this chapter "Arthropods Shouldn't Exist" (thank you, Wikipedia) to include all manner of arachnids and other horrifying types of creatures you would find in an Indiana Jones movie. It makes total sense to me that spiders would have their own classification since they instil a kind of terror in me that warrants their very own category. It's probably a good thing that I will never preside as ruler over any country with a nuclear arsenal, since ballistic missiles would always be my weapon of choice when a spider invaded my home. Instead, I always have to settle for an old shoe or any large blunt object that I will never have to touch ever again. Sometimes it is easier just to move out. I've had more addresses in life than the Littlest Hobo.

As if it weren't bad enough that insects are gross, they seem to instinctively thrive on being as irritating as possible, like it's part of their genetic makeup and natural design. Always showing up where they're not wanted, or in the case of flies, buzzing around your head and testing your sanity like some sadistic form of torture. How long can you endure the loud buzzing in your ear and swat at them to no avail before running hysterically back into the house or some other form of shelter? And what kind of twit spends all day flying around someone's head? What are they trying to prove? Is that how you would choose to spend your time if you had wings? Actually, I can think of a couple of people who probably would.

One of my proudest moments in life was the time a large horsefly was buzzing around my head and I backhanded it so hard in mid-air that it fell and tumbled across the ground dead as a doornail. I stood there for a couple of minutes, marvelling at how badass I was and hoping there were other flies around who witnessed it. "You SEE?!" I screamed. "This is what happens! Tell all your friends! YOU MIGHT BE NEXT!"

The fact that some people eat chocolate covered ants and other insects as if they're some kind of delicacy is enough to make me gag. Sometimes I wonder if there is anything people *won't* eat. Hey why not a nice big bag of salt and vinegar dog crap while you're at it? Finding a bug in my food is like the best diet ever as far as I'm concerned, since it turns me off eating for so long I end up on intravenous. There *was* that one time that one landed in my wine and I drank it anyway, but I feel like the alcohol probably acted as a kind of sanitizer and I was not about to dump out good wine just because some brain-dead fruit fly overestimated his piloting skills.

The only reason insects have so many eyes and legs and spare parts is because God knew everyone would constantly be trying to kill them. Ever notice how often you don't get them on the first try and they keep stumbling along on the rest of their limbs? Ugh... I hate them with such a fiery passion I don't even want to talk about this anymore. This chapter got me all worked up and I need to go lay down for a while. I'll talk to you later.

chapter 13:
stuff

People are always coming up to me in the street or the grocery store or whatever and asking me for advice on how to live life to the fullest, and I have learned to use my uncanny resemblance to Oprah as a platform and opportunity to help others. One of the best pieces of advice I can give them, and you, is to get rid of all your "stuff".

The clamouring for material wealth and *things* is nothing short of an epidemic in this world, and the psychology of this overwhelming desire people have to acquire inanimate objects is all very fascinating, albeit misguided. It goes back as far as recorded history, and mankind has been conditioned to believe the more material possessions they have, the happier they will be, and the more "success" they have achieved. Even cavepeople gloated about how many rocks they had or how big their cave was. Which begs the question: "How much is enough?" There are only so many closets and garages you can fill with your boxes and bags before you end up on an episode of *Hoarders*. And what is the point? When you die, nobody is going to care how much crap was in your house and be all "Wow, they really had a great life! Look at all their crap!" In fact, all you are doing is creating a mess for your family to clean up after you bite the dust, and as we've already established, that could be any day now. It's not like you can take any of it with you. Well you can try, but it would make for a very awkward funeral. Tossing a rose or a handful of dirt as a ritual is one thing, but nobody wants the priest to be interrupted by the beeping noise of a large truck backing up and dumping all your tea pots and Tupperware into the hole all over your casket so that you can have it with you while you decay.

I'm not suggesting you keep your home bare to the point of being sterile, but you should make it a habit to pick up random objects around your house once in a while and ask yourself whether they are making you happy or serve some purpose. I do this with my housekeeper often even though he is quite heavy, and though the answer is almost always no, I have learned over the years that one rule of thumb for keeping things is to ask yourself if it's capable of hiring a lawyer. I also try to keep as few things as possible that will only serve to collect dust, since nobody around here seems to understand that dusting should be done regularly even though that's what they're paid for.

Also, if you insist on collecting stuff, try to keep it somewhat organized so that you always know where to find it. People constantly run out to the store to replace stuff they already own simply because they can't find the stuff that's buried underneath a pile of other stuff. When you have time, use a software program like Excel to list in detail and categorize all your stuff in a spreadsheet and indicate the coordinates in your home where the objects can be located. Use letters and numbers to label all your shelves so you can refer to them easily. That way, when your husband or wife yells out "Honey, have you seen my scissors with the yellow handle?" You can be all "Why yes dear, they are located on shelf G2 of storage closet B" and they'll be like "Thanks! Omg I love how organized we are!" And you'll be like "Omg me too!" And you'll both be all happy. I've probably just saved your marriage.

I suggest trying to limit yourself to only a few important keepsakes that hold special meaning or real value to you, like some pictures of special moments in time, good books that have enlightened you like this one, or letters from family and friends written back when they still liked you. The less you own in this life, the less importance you will place on owning stuff, and the more you will care about things of lasting value and maybe finally doing something to contribute to the world around you while you still can, so people don't show up to your funeral one day looking at your coffin like another box full of useless junk too.

chapter 14:
money

They say money is the root of all evil. I feel it would be far more accurate to say that if evil were a weed, the root wouldn't be money, but more likely a person buried in the mud holding the money with the weeds protruding from their greedy hands and probably out of their nostrils too. People are basically the root from which everything undesirable on the earth grows and flourishes. Maybe I should quit writing books and write Hallmark greeting cards instead.

Money is merely a tool for trading that goes back as far as biblical times and can neither be good nor evil, in my opinion, but is grossly mistreated and mismanaged by the vast majority of the world's population, so I'm going to give you some tips on how to be a little more financially wise. Feel free to pass these lessons on to your kids as well if you haven't already sold them.

If you feel like you don't make enough money, you can start by asking your boss to begin paying you in five dollar bills. It will give you a new appreciation for pay day and make it feel like winning the lottery every time. You can take it all home and put it in a big pile on the bed and roll around in it naked to satisfy the money-hungry troll in you inherent to humanity.

The next and most important tip I can give you about money is to give it away, especially if you are struggling to pay your bills. I know you think you'll starve, or lose your car, but you'll get back many times more than what you give, believe me, and you'll find that you hold it less tightly. This philosophy applies to pretty much anything you hold too tightly, including your wine glass, so I will hold that for you for the duration of the chapter.

There is a sense of entitlement in today's culture and a massive overindulgence resulting in household debt of epidemic proportions. The invention of the credit card was a great day for the devil, I'll tell you that right now. The first time somebody charged a big screen television to their Visa, he sat back and lit a cigarette and said "Oh man, I am going to save so much time ruining people's lives now. I'm just. . . so happy right now. I'm so happy!" And a glistening tear of joy rolled down his cheek before sizzling due to the scalding hot evilness emanating from his stupid, evil face. Every time you charged something you couldn't afford, he was laughing at you, just so you know. And not just a little giggle either. I mean like sometimes laughing hard enough that he snorted and was embarrassed.

Where did this amazing logic of spending money that doesn't exist come from, I wonder? This is all the rage with governments now too. They call it "stimulating the economy" by basically running up a 500 billion dollar bill that nobody can pay. That's fantastic. I feel over-stimulated just talking about it. The world is now run by spoiled children who didn't hear the word "no" often enough. Well it's one of my favourite words, so get used to seeing it a LOT in this book, and on any wedding invitations you send me too for that matter.

The best thing you can do for your children financially is teach them about credit cards and the danger of debt. Or not have children in the first place. Whichever method works best for you. This is another area where schools should be stepping up to the plate too and teaching something of major importance in life instead of how to dissect a frog or giant grasshopper and postulate theories on what they ate based on what they find in their turd. I guess those lessons are applicable to daily living somehow. Like maybe if they ever need to do a post-mortem on the pet they charged to their credit card and then couldn't afford to bring to the vet when it got sick.

I do hope you feel like you're getting your money's worth out of this book at least. It's probably on your Visa now too. Or maybe you downloaded it for free, in which case you just wasted all your time reading this chapter since you obviously have no use for money and just steal everything you want like an immoral, thieving savage. Serves you right.

chapter 15:
philosophy for
dummies

You're probably thinking that by the title of this chapter I'm implying that you're some kind of dummy, but let me assure you, I already established that many chapters ago.

I think it's time we got into the real guts of existence and self-awareness before getting any deeper into our examination of the human condition and how to navigate our short time in this life as we currently know it, whether you believe there will be something after it or not. This includes various questions such as: "Why am I me, and not someone else?" And "How can I be sure I am me and not merely an observer of me with an inside perspective, and if that were the case, then who am I if I'm not who I thought I was?" Hold on I need another glass of wine.

Okay I'm back. I'm sorry what was I saying? Oh yeah, perspective. I don't know about you, but I have often had a great deal of success enduring an unpleasant situation by entertaining the possibility that I am not actually me and that it's happening to someone else and I'm just basically watching a bad movie or something. If you think about it, how do I really know I'm me? "I think, therefore I am?" Is it because I feel when I touch, or because I taste? Pain would be a great indicator that I am really me, because it hurts, and who would choose to feel pain voluntarily if they were someone other than the person who is feeling it? Are you following me so far? Or am I actually you, and you're me asking you if you're following me? If that were the case, and I am you and you're me, let me take this opportunity to say that you should probably seek professional help.

As the famous Socratic paradox goes: I know one thing, that I know nothing. There is something to be said for acknowledging the limits of what we know for absolute certain, though I am not necessarily suggesting everyone should go around proclaiming how dense they are, even though some of you probably should. Sometimes it feels like there is no point in the study of anything since nothing can be known for sure, and one person's belief of what is true is not always true and merely a matter of their perspective. Like famous philosopher Bill Clinton once said: "It depends on what the definition of 'is' is."

What if two plus two isn't really four, but it's like, five or something? People assume mathematical laws are "true" just because people called four "four" instead of "five" and made up a rule on what the definition of four is. If I invent my own mathematics and decide that it equals five and you disagree with me, I'll tell you right now that you're going to flunk my math course. That's assuming I'm actually me and even give a damn.

Let me give you an example. Just the other day at a department store, I picked up a certain item for an advertised price of $10.99 plus applicable taxes. When I got to the cash register to pay for my item, I postulated to the cashier that perhaps the way she read the sign was not the same way that I did and that it really amounted to half that much, and asked her if she could prove what she was seeing through her eyes was any more correct than what I saw through mine.

How could she prove that is what the sign said? Just saying "that's what I see" or "that's what it says" doesn't prove anything, and even if it did, who is to say what $10.99 even MEANS? A very intense philosophical debate ensued between me, the cashier, the store manager, and eventually store security. By the end of it all, they ended up charging me more than the original price and banning me from the store for life. But they were never really able to prove anything I said was false in a way that was satisfactory to me. I'm also fairly certain that everyone involved was invigorated by the discussion considering how passionately they were speaking, and that's what I'm here for.

Another area of interest in the philosophical arena is the nature of good and evil, the knowledge of which I believe is naturally present in all of mankind aside from the existence of any mental disorders like those exhibited by insects that we discussed earlier. I don't buy into the whole idea that upbringing and environmental factors are to blame for a person's evil nature, even if it does stunt their growth and start them off on the wrong foot. Many people endure horrible circumstances and still grow up to find their way and know the difference between right and wrong.

I know what you're going to say. Just like in my math course where two plus two equals five, what if in your morality course what I think is wrong is actually right and it's all a matter of perspective? I'm not going to let you drag me into some kind of circular argument that can't possibly lead to any positive outcome, especially since we already established I might actually be you, and end up punching myself in your face.

Let's change the subject.

chapter 16: thinking

I think this is a great opportunity to segue into a discussion on one of my very most favourite pastimes in life, and that is thinking. I'm sure you can tell by the previous chapter that I engage in a great deal of it, much to the profit of the academic community, and I suggest that you try it from time to time as an alternative to some of the more common recreational activities nowadays that produce very little in the way of personal growth, such as water skiing or pole dancing.

I know that a certain degree of thinking is involved in any activity, but that's not the kind of thinking I'm talking about here. I'm talking about the really deep kind of thinking, where one thinks for the sake of thinking, thinking on purpose, and generating thoughts that provoke even deeper thoughts and all your neurons are firing to the point where it seems like something is burning and some kind of revelatory explosion is taking place. And no, I'm not talking about a stroke, though I am definitely smelling burnt toast right now.

A long burst of purposeful thinking in solitude is a very healthy activity with sometimes very lasting and tangible results. I know that my life has switched directions numerous times because of certain thinking sessions that brought new ideas to light and helped me see a new and better path for my future.

Right about now you're thinking: "So how do I go about this whole thinking thing? And if I'm thinking that question, doesn't that mean I already know how?" Well, each person is different and it takes practice to find which are the right circumstances and environments for your best thinking. I do a lot of *my* best thinking in the shower for example, and though I eventually emerge looking like a giant raisin, I can seldom get to my computer fast enough to record all of my ideas. Driving is another good one for me, and I feel like that is rather unique, since other drivers often don't appear to be thinking at all. Above all, though, my best thinking is probably done in the candlelight in an open room where I can pace back and forth like a mad scientist. It is the fire in which most of this book was forged, but to each their own.

I believe there is a solution to every problem that exists that can be revealed through thinking and meditation. That's something to think about that you can start with. I bet you believe there are certain things going on in your life right now that are like an adversary who can't be out-thought, but thinking is like anything else; consistent practice yields inevitable improvement and results. You can't learn to play the violin if you don't try, and the same goes with using your brain. Granted, some people could spend 20 years trying to be a violinist and still suck at it, so the same kind of common sense applies here, where one must at least start out with some degree of talent with their brain before they spend too much time with it. Like most other chapters in this book, this one isn't for everyone.

There are times that I wished it were possible to have a career doing nothing but thinking, so I could simply get lost in thought without interruption and still survive. I am currently looking for investors in my think tank to make this a reality. Something else to think about. I know I could produce answers to some of the greatest problems plaguing society today, like why nobody else seems to think about thinking. There is a great deal of spontaneous, instinctual action taking place in society without any prior thought. Look at the way you're dressed today for example.

Thinking also has enormous power and influence on our dreams. Getting your mind trained to think right thoughts before bedtime can yield very pleasurable experiences throughout the night. Please get your mind out of the gutter because that's not even what I'm talking about. Clearly we got nowhere with chapter 9. I'm talking about fantastical journeys where one can live out the jobs or experiences they are obviously incapable of manifesting otherwise, and wake up feeling like it all really happened, setting them on course to eventually make it reality. Unfortunately, it works in both directions, and wielding no control over what we think can have disastrous repercussions, both as far as nightmares or saying something stupid and losing all your friends, or your job, or both simultaneously and worrying ourselves into an unproductive mess. Thinking, like all things, requires discipline.

When my mind was younger and undisciplined, my thoughts got me into a world of trouble. I choose to look back on it as though my mind was like a powerful firehose turned on full blast and I was trying to control it and hang on, flying around all over the place with it and knocking people over and drowning them instead of using it to put out fires. I've always been this good with metaphors though, that will never change.

Once I got older and wiser, I learned how to handle my proverbial hose with greater care and discipline and went on to write self-help books like this one that teach millions of others how to handle their hose too without accidentally drowning themselves. Can't do much thinking while we're dead now can we. Or can we. I don't like using question marks when I don't really want anyone to answer, by the way. That will be a clue for you going forward.

chapter 17:
music

It is a universal love, and a form of communication that can be felt and understood in any language the world over. Nothing evokes an emotional response in everyone like the sound of music, or can change a person's mood as quickly. One moment you're sticking your head in the oven, and then the right song comes on that gets you snapping your fingers and tapping your feet and suddenly you have a whole new lease on life and anything is possible and you pull your head out of the oven so fast you bang it on the top but it's ok because you're alive and nobody was looking and even if they were, you were only cleaning it ok?!

Song selection can change the entire way a day progresses, and for this reason, I suggest managing and organizing playlists of various types of songs which can then be used to manipulate your mood accordingly when the need arises instead of resorting to medication. Though it is simply not a matter of creating the playlists, one must possess the strength and courage to actually listen to them. It is a rather difficult exercise to select your Happy Playlist when feeling sad, for example, even when you know the result will be beneficial. I believe the key to succeeding at this is to first start to sing one of the happy songs aloud and allow it to get "stuck in your head" as it were. The right empowering song and a strong cup of coffee is always the recipe for an energetic and productive morning for me. I mean the kind of song that gets you so riled up that anything feels possible, even being able to sing!

Speaking of singing, we should talk a bit about suitable environments. I like to choose a venue with favourable acoustics where I can hear my long, belting notes reverberating around me and where I can explore my upper whistle register like Mariah Carey. Personally, I find the shower or one of the stairwells of my building preferable. There were times I'm pretty sure I could have sold tickets at the door, especially for the shower. Most people like singing while driving but that is predictable and ordinary, and will never lead to stardom.

The vocal abilities necessary for great singing are a blessing that can be bestowed upon people by God alone, so it's a shame that there are so many people who think they were recipients but were clearly left off the list. I for one see this as more evidence of God's sense of humour, along with the invention of karaoke and alcohol.

Perhaps this is why people who are famous for their gift have long been revered and idolized by the millions of peons who can only dream. What a magnificent thing it is to hear professional singers' voices soar like a biological instrument, making us weep with empathy and identify with the poorly written but pertinent lyrics about rejection and misery.

Songs instantly transport us to the times and places we first heard them and preserve those memories for us and make them accessible whenever we feel the need to wallow in despair.

I feel like I've gotten off track here somewhere in this chapter. Maybe it's because I'm listening to "I Have Nothing" by Whitney Houston while I'm writing it. See what I mean about the influential power of music? I could have chosen one of her happier songs like "I Wanna Dance With Somebody" and this would have all ended up being a little more perky. I actually have a lot in common with Whitney since I am also a hot mess who loves Jesus and will probably end up drowning in a bath tub some day. I think we're done here.

chapter 18:
lol

They say that laughter is the best medicine, and I couldn't agree more, unless you have Ebola or something, in which case there are probably better medicines to try, but the benefits of laughter should never be ignored in any situation.

People so often wait to "look back and laugh" at something horrible that happened to them, but if you're going to end up laughing at it later, why not start now? I can assure you there are people laughing at your life choices in the present rather than waiting till later, so you might as well join them instead of crying about it. I often cry at my mistakes, but it is only from laughing so hard, like the time I nearly choked to death on my Smarties in a movie theatre. The irony is that I was already throwing my head back in laughter with a mouthful of Smarties in the first place which caused me to violently gag on them, thus inducing more laughter, much to the entertainment of the surrounding movie goers who were also laughing. It's a happy memory for me and important life lesson about how I could have been hysterically fearful of my impending death and motioning for someone to give me the Heimlich Manoeuvre instead of just enjoying the moment and a genuine, hearty laugh which is hard to come by.

There is, however, much debate over the appropriateness of laughter at certain times, like at a funeral for example. It's interesting though how this taboo in itself can cause some of us to burst into fits of laughter simply because we're not supposed to. It's like the time I was asked to deliver a eulogy and started with "A guy walks into a doctor's office." Mourners are a tough crowd, let me tell you. I was just standing there like "Is this thing even on?"

It can also make people feel as though they are not being taken seriously. For example, while pouring my heart out into this fine work of literature it is obviously my hope to be regarded with respect as an author and enlightener (I like that word), and not to be laughed at. Laughing is permissible while reading this book, but only when appropriate, which is almost never. "Enlightener" is going to look really good on my resume.

Another issue with laughter can be sincerity. How many times has somebody replied to one of your texts with "lol" when you knew for absolute certain they were not laughing? They were probably not even smiling. This is especially annoying during an argument when they add "lol" at the end of their own half-witted comment to make it seem like they don't really care. Like "oh hahaha I'm not as worked up about this situation as you and I'm over here laughing and I'm so cool and whatever." Don't make me gag on my Smarties.

Which brings us to all the different abbreviations to denote fits of laughter online. Like ROTFLMAO. Are you really rolling on the floor laughing? I suppose it does happen, but those moments are rare. Like shark attack rare. Whenever somebody writes that, I picture them sitting in front of their computer with a blank stare, suffering from some kind of psychoneurosis.

Laughter can also have kind of an evil connotation to it. You'll notice that most notorious villains in all the Disney movies laugh uncontrollably, especially after doing something particularly sinister that's not even really that funny. I firmly believe that growing up with that kind of influence has affected many of us who behave in that fashion on occasion. I always imagine that my anaesthesiologist will start to laugh like Maleficent just as he puts me under for an operation. I know I would if that were my job.

Speaking of medically induced laughter, it reminds me of the time my dentist gave me laughing gas for an unusually deep cavity he was attempting to repair. Now that was a good time. I never would have thought I'd find having holes drilled into my head so comical. If only all visits to the dentist were that enjoyable, I would have been a much better and more frequent customer. Maybe we'll revisit dentistry in a later chapter.

On that note, since this book is supposed to cover natural disasters, I think we'll move onto one that's most suitable after a discussion on laughter: romantic love.

chapter 19:
romantic love

I feel like broaching this subject is akin to walking on broken glass. I shall endeavour to tread lightly, and carefully. That being said, if you thought that David Copperfield making the Statue of Liberty disappear was an amazing illusion, it pales in comparison to the illusion of romantic love.

I know what you're going to say: I'm just another bitter, jaded person whose heart was broken and now I am cynical on the subject of love. While it might be true that I had an unpleasant experience with someone who shall remain nameless (or rename Mainless), I feel that only further qualifies me to write this chapter with an educated perspective. Now stop interrupting me.

Romantic love is like a narcotic that humans are genetically predisposed to think they need for survival in life. Whenever their current supply runs out, they desperately seek another, and another, until one day they are cut off from a particularly potent supply and go mad with rage and withdrawal symptoms, making them practically unbearable to be around. And let's face it, some of you weren't that fun to start with.

People cut off from their love supply also behave in a similar way to heroin addicts in that they stop caring about how they dress or present themselves, they're always sad, and they settle for meaningless sex to procure more of the drug and feel better even though that is like a cheaper no name brand that doesn't work as well.

Every once in a while, you'll encounter a strong, independent person who has broken the mould and leads a content life without turning to romance to feel alive and fulfilled, but the majority out there still thrive on all the high highs and low, low, *lows* that accompany it.

Granted, it is a passionate thing that has inspired some great movies and music, and I'm not even going to try to tell you how to break the addiction. I feel like that would be a futile exercise like when we talked about dieting in chapter 5.

It just doesn't work. What I *will* do is help you better prepare for the inevitable demise of your current relationship, and also help those of you who aren't in one be happier alone until you find another supplier, or die.

First, let's talk about your impending breakup. Sure, everything may seem great right now and you're still buying each other flowers and being insufferable around your friends, talking about how great your significant other is, but in due time, all that is going to change. It's like a mathematical formula. Nay, it is like a lifeform with a finite existence. Love is alive, and just like plants and animals, it dies. Some live for many years, some for days. Like a flower without water, it ends up crusty, shrivelled and dead.

So if love is alive, why do I say it's an illusion? Well the illusion comes into play because of how people perceive the love they're experiencing. They believe it's magical and indestructible. Don't deny it! When you're in love you think you found the only unicorn that ever existed. But it's actually just a plain old workhorse like everyone else's that eventually gets tired and just stands around the farm expelling manure or breaks a leg and has to be shot. We cry over how it used to prance around, full of energy when it was youthful and new, but we can't go back in time. This is when the addicts go get a new horse and show it off to everyone, claiming it's even better than the last one and more fun to ride. I'll admit these metaphors may be getting out of hand.

So how do we know when our relationship is about to end? Well there are a few red flags we can watch for. Let's take a look at a scene from a play I wrote called *A Streetcar Named Divorce*, whose successful run on Broadway was due largely to the fact that everyone can relate to having their heart smashed to pieces. This particular scene is from the very end of the third act, when we see signs the relationship of the two main characters, Burt and Harriet, may be starting to break down:

[SCENE: Burt and Harriet are lying in bed. Burt reaches over to turn the lamp off on the nightstand while Harriet sighs and stares at the ceiling.]

BURT: Goodnight Harriet.
HARRIET: Goodnight? What's good about it? You're abysmal. It's the only word that comes to mind when I think of you. Abysmal. Because being married to you is like being trapped in an abyss of nothingness with no hope of escape and the mere thought of waking up beside you one more time makes me long for death.

[CURTAIN.]

So what do we do when our magic carpet ride ends just as we were going over the Grand Canyon? Have your grieving period if you need to, but I was hoping more that you were taking notes in the last chapter and would learn to laugh at things like this. You're about to find out that most of your family and friends probably didn't like who you were seeing anyway, so go ahead and act as relieved as they are.

As for those of you who are alone, congratulations. You're already way ahead of everyone else and only have one problem to deal with instead of two. The trick here is to enjoy the friends and family who have been present in storms instead of just fair weather. Aside from that, alone time is harder to come by than you think and should be used effectively. It's only when people can't have it that they start to realize its value. People with no romantic attachment can achieve great things with all the time they have for self-improvement and reflection on things of spiritual importance, unlike the unicorn they thought they had that ended up at the glue factory.

I think that's enough time spent on romance. Boy if I had a dollar for every time I said that. And speaking of time, let's spend some time now talking about time in the next chapter.

chapter 20:
time

The world is obsessed with time, and with good reason. Our lives are basically made up of it, and consist of all the seconds allotted to us, whatever that number may be. I have a very large clock over my writing desk that is a constant reminder to me that my time here is fixed and each tick of the second hand could be the last one I experience for various reasons. I find these classic analog clocks aesthetically pleasing as a decoration more than anything else though, because I'm more of a digital person really. I'm too deep in thought and distracted when people ask me the time and I get the hands all mixed up and end up telling them the time in

Bosnia or wherever instead of here. It's all part of my charm I guess.

It's fascinating that even though our lives consist of time, everyone is constantly engaging in any activity that will distract them from the passage of time and make it go faster. Almost all recreational activities, and anything that people find "fun" is a distraction from time. That is why people think time is moving slower at work when they don't enjoy their jobs. Or why a watched pot never boils, because let's face it, watching a pot is not very fun, depending on who you put in it.

Obviously, boredom or unpleasant situations are keys to feeling that life is lasting longer. I remember once watching a documentary on the ocean called *Ocean Planet* that was so boring I actually became fascinated by how bored I was and continued to watch only for this reason. This show was not about interesting fishes or ocean life, it was just about the ocean itself, and for a while I believed I had discovered the secret to making time stand still. You've probably had a similar experience reading this book.

Since we have a fixed and uncertain amount of time at our disposal, I suggest getting into a strict habit of writing down important uses of our time for the next day before going to bed. If you don't plan your day, somebody else will. I know, you could die before tomorrow arrives and then making your schedule would have been wasted time, but frankly you probably wouldn't have been doing anything else productive with those few minutes anyway.

Scheduling is imperative to being one of the lead runners in the race against time. You go into the day knowing how you'll make the most of it and which tasks must be completed instead of wasting hours either wondering what you should do with your time or following somebody else who knows what they're doing. Bosses and leaders are usually good time managers since that is essentially what they do in life: decide how other people will use time. If you've been sitting at your desk whining about how slow the day's progressing instead of making the most of each hour, you probably shouldn't hold your breath for a promotion at this point. In fact, you should probably be fired. Not just from your job. From everything.

You'll notice as you get older that time seems to pass more quickly with each year, since a year represents an increasingly smaller percentage of your life experience. A year is a very long time to a ten-year-old because it's ten percent of their total existence. That's why kids get so cranky and bored often, because everything appears to take an eternity from their perspective. I can think of no better disciplinary measure for an unruly child than to force them to sit through *Ocean Planet*. No need to ground them for weeks. It's only a few hours for you, but for them it's like being trapped in Hell till the end of time. I guarantee they'll come out of it having learned their lesson.

I probably spend more time thinking about time than I should, which you could say is a waste of time, and I can't get the time back I already spent on this chapter, so let's just leave it at that and I'll see you tomorrow, unless one of us runs out of time.

chapter 21: sleep

Let's talk about that mysterious state of being that recharges our bodies as if we're all a bunch of walking batteries that hold less and less charge as we age and eventually end up in a landfill. Sleep, like happiness, is elusive depending on your frame of mind, but not entirely impossible to acquire with the right training. The inability to engage in this otherwise catatonic waste of time is commonly referred to as insomnia, or as I like to call it: the resistance movement.

I'm not here to recruit anyone, and frankly you have enough problems, so instead I'm going to give you the necessary tools to get the 14 hours of sleep that you obviously require to maintain some level of coherence and ability to function.

It's been my experience that smarter people have a lot more difficulty entering their daily coma than those with less going on upstairs, if you know what I mean, since an active and stimulated mind is one of the foremost reasons why sleep eludes people. If you're not sure what I mean, you can probably skip this chapter. I sometimes wondered why it was necessary to design our bodies with a dependency on intermittent unconsciousness until I realized that if I were God I would definitely force us to pass out and shut up every day too.

Let's say you're lying in bed at night and your mind starts to wander all over the place, examining in great detail everything that could possibly go wrong in the future, everything you didn't get done today, instability and suffering in parts of the world, the threat of global nuclear war, your health, my health, what we'll wear to that dreaded social function, and all the smart comebacks you now have for that argument that took place three weeks ago. It's time to exercise some discipline over your mind to bring some calm to the stormy waters crashing around in your head.

You may want to try the age-old technique of counting sheep jumping over a fence. Although, to be honest, I'm not entirely sure how sheep became the animal of choice for this.

Of all the animals that have existed since the beginning of time, which bright-light decided sheep were best suited for fence jumping? When is the last time you saw one jump a fence? Can they even jump that high? If they even jump at all, they'd never make it over *my* fence, I'll tell you that right now. And even if they did, I'd be waiting on the other side and they would rue the day they ever tried to leave my farm. That sheep would end up back in the yard and naked too after I sheered their disloyal ass and made a sweater out of it. At least I know what I'll wear now. How did I get left to look after this farm anyway? As if I don't have enough problems. Pretty sure egg and milk production is down this quarter and I don't know how I'm supposed to address the problem and count the sheep at the same time. Where are all of my farmhands? This is so typical. It's almost 3:00 a.m. and I only have four hours left to round up all the animals and put together a marketing strategy for the Dairy Processors Association and still get enough sleep to function at my real job tomorrow.

You know what, just forget about the friggin' sheep. I want you to relax and imagine that your mind is a big, blank, empty, black vacuum; completely devoid of any substance. That shouldn't be too difficult for you. Each thought that enters your mind is a shape or image that appears in the vacuum and sails towards the black hole that is now forming. Not even light can escape a black hole, so imagine that there is no thought that can remain in your big, spacious head without being sucked into oblivion. I practice this technique often while people are talking to me and I can tell you it works. Remain ever so still in your bed, so as not to crack the window from behind which you are viewing your personal galaxy, and keep all thoughts far from it so it doesn't break or you'll be blown out into space. I'm pretty sure I don't need to tell you what happens to the human body in a vacuum. Needless to say you might better have stayed on the farm. At least there your head wouldn't have imploded as your decompressed body floats into a black hole. And you were worried about what to wear?

Maybe you should just try to do something very boring for an hour or two before bed. Check the television guide and see if *Ocean Planet* is on or something. Remember to use the timer function on your television though. I'm sure you've seen enough horror movies to know what might crawl out of it during the night. Undead beings coming through the screen while you are half-conscious and vulnerable is not conducive to a good night's sleep.

I like to do logic puzzles in bed because it helps to tire out the mind much in the same way this book does, making me less able to conjure up thoughts of all the horrors that befall the average lifespan. You could also try something repetitive, like knitting. I mean what else are you going to do with all that wool?

chapter 22:
autumn

What a grand reprieve is autumn from the harsh conditions or busyness of lesser seasons. Autumn is the artist's season, in my opinion, when life slows down, cools down, and everywhere you look is like a painting. Unless of course you live somewhere bleak like the desert or tundra with no leaves/hope. I refer more to the Canadian or North Eastern American autumn, and you haven't lived until you've experienced one. You might be one of the millions of sun worshippers who loves your summer activities and flowers, but by the end of this chapter, hopefully you'll have a new appreciation for one of God's greatest masterpieces.

If you're a parent, one good reason to love the fall is that it's time for all of your annoying kids to go back to school and give you some peace and quiet to enjoy the colours. If you're a kid, I guess it's a reason to hate the fall, but look at it this way: you're going to learn how to read in school, otherwise you would miss out on books like this one that teach you to love the fall for the same reason you hate it. I think I just created my first paradox. Don't count on learning *that* in school. Who gave you this book anyway, kid? It's for adults only. Good thing you can't read yet. Not exactly like I had a responsive audience before anyway. Maybe they can't read either... Hello?

Fall scenery provides an inspiring atmosphere to reflect on your year and contemplate life and I firmly believe the cool and beautiful surroundings have a slowing effect on the moment. Leaves float down streams, fires crackle and smoke to keep you warm in the evening chill, making you defend your personal space with less vigour. In fact, let's cuddle.

In the summer everything and everyone is so busy. You can't even grocery shop without someone driving over your toes with their rickety shopping cart. It's hot and muggy outside and everyone is cranky and stressed. There's traffic and construction and everything involves a big tent and a barbecue with some big disgusting sausages on it. "Oh look, it's summer! Let me throw a big sloppy piece of meat on the barbie like some kind of ritual sacrifice to the sun gods and we can all congregate around it and sweat!" That's what all the summer people say.

Autumn is a gift to photographers like emotional turmoil is to poets. Even an amateur with a cheap camera can shine like a professional. You'll never take an ugly picture in the fall. Unless it's a selfie. I'm only kidding. Boy, that was a knee-slapper. Just trying to lighten the mood around here, okay? I sure wish I had chosen to write this book in the fall. I might feel a bit less discouraged. I could toast marshmallows on the campfire between chapters and roll around in the leaves. Hold on, I'm just going to jot down some quick notes here for my next book: *Making The Most of an Insufferable Experience Like Writing a Book.*

There are so many places in the world with perpetual winter or summer, where it is cold and snowy year-round, or hot and sunny. I wish there was somewhere in the world with an eternal autumn and large forest where the leaves never stopped falling. I would have a large log home there and I would sit on the porch daily under a blanket, reading and smoking a pipe or whatever you're supposed to do on a porch in the woods. I suppose then it wouldn't be special, but perhaps I will conjure this image tonight instead of the black hole. You know, just to mix it up a little.

chapter 23: tornadoes

Ahh, yes. Tornadoes. The most terrifying and ominous of all natural disasters. Nothing compares to the sight of such a monstrosity descending from the sky above, and steadily hovering through the darkness towards you. In my lifetime I have had, at last count, 1,293 tornado nightmares, which obviously qualifies me as an expert in the field. While other people are counting sheep or dissecting their day in bed, I am over here in my tornado research van awaiting the inevitable storm.

So what is a tornado exactly? Well, it's basically a big spinning, spiraling vortex of doom that rotates and comes downward to dispose of anything in its path. If you want to see a demonstration of how they form, I suggest you go flush your toilet. In fact, you can think of tornadoes as God up in the sky hitting a giant flush handle on all your hopes and dreams.

Most people think that all the destructive force of a tornado is limited to its wind speeds at hundreds of miles per hour, but in fact, a lot of structures are destroyed by the rapid change in pressure as they pass by, causing them to explode. This phenomenon is not only limited to structures. The same intense pressure can also occur in a person's head and cause their eyes to bulge out. That is why whenever you see somebody standing beside a tornado, they almost always look surprised.

Most experts advise heading to the basement as quickly as possible for safety when a tornado is approaching. This may be good in theory, but hasn't worked out so well for me in the past. And not just because I don't have a basement. Many of the tornadoes I've survived in nightmares have destroyed other people's houses where basements did not provide sufficient protection. I've dreamt of some people's homes (like Mainless's for example) being destroyed over and over and over again, basement and all, smashed into a trillion pieces and blown into the dark night sky and me along with it, never to be seen or heard from again. I wonder what that means.

There is a very small window of opportunity to escape at the first signs of an imminent encounter with a tornado. You do not want to be caught off guard when they reach a certain distance and trajectory. One guy I know of was too busy taking a selfie in front of one to avoid being sucked in and flung into the heavens, though he did have enough time to post it on Instagram before coming back down. That one got a lot of likes.

I'm not sure what would ever possess somebody to live in what is known as "Tornado Alley" in North America, or Kansas City for that matter, where tornadoes are a way of life. My fear of them is probably akin to the person who fears flying all their life and finally works up the courage to get on a plane, which then flies into the side of a mountain. I know if I am ever in the same town as a tornado, it will head straight for me. You won't want to be around me when that happens. And since I fear both flying and tornadoes, it will be an ironic death for me.

I believe that tornadoes are a great illustration of how problems approach us. Everything appears to be fine across the landscape as we're moving through our daily routines, all is running smoothly, day after day, and then just when you're getting a little too comfortable with all the calmness, the sky is turning a vomit green and darkening, the sun is retreating in the middle of the day, and the rumbling of an incoming problem gets louder and louder until finally there's cows and transports flying all over the place and debris from destroyed buildings and wine glasses rocketing sidewards and hitting people right between the eyes while you're stuck under a bridge, desperately clinging to something and hoping you can hang on till it passes, but you can't, and you let go and let out a blood-curdling scream as you're swept up with everyone else and sucked into the funnel and blown out the top like a frog in a wood chipper. No wonder the subconscious likes to render life's troubles into these types of dreams. I'm going to be ready for the next one though. I've taken a tip from the movie *Twister* and I'm going to fasten all kinds of balls to myself before I go to sleep that will fly around inside the tornado and collect useful data so I can better predict future problems. I'll let you know what I find out.

chapter 24:
youth

There's an old saying, but I'm still too young to know what it is. The world celebrates youth and the beauty and energy it represents more and more in today's culture instead of the wisdom and experience that comes with age. Just another sign that this planet is spinning backwards and hurtling towards its doom if you ask me.

I am first to admit that being young has its own challenges and experience. I have the battle scars to prove it, and while some people are proclaiming how they long to be twenty again and relive those years, I experience random gratitude that there's currently no technology available that could ever force me back in time.

Virtually all people learn things in life the same way, which is of course, the hard way: running headlong into a self-made disaster to find out it's not how to handle things in the future should you survive to try again. It's amazing that our society worships this state of perpetual foolishness simply because of the physical vitality and social glamour that accompanies it. Perhaps it is that greater sense of freedom to make mistakes that causes people to long for their youth, but let me assure you, you're still free to make as many as you want. Just look at your recent Facebook posts.

Going back even further to when we were little kids and had nothing to worry about except playing with our toys while somebody else cooked and cleaned for us makes a little more sense. But even then, we were subject to the whims of other adults. Who would give up their freedom to go back to that maximum security playpen? And newsflash: getting adults to cook and clean for you is not exclusive to childhood, except now you can buy all the Lego you want and nobody's going to tell you when it's time to stop playing with it and go to bed. Your housekeeper can try, but the difference is we can talk back to other adults now and they still have to pick up our toys.

One thing I do miss about childhood is playing games. It's very difficult nowadays to convince other adults to play something like Hide-And-Go-Seek, especially once you get a reputation for never going to look for anyone after they hide. This used to be my go-to solution when hosting a dinner party and now the suggestion is virtually ignored.

And what about tag? "You're it!" Running around the playground with the sounds of children's laughter. Adult tag sounds a little more like "You're it!"

"No, YOU'RE it!"

"No bitch, you are definitely IT and GET THE HELL OUT OF MY HOUSE!"

One of the greatest challenges in becoming an adult is to let go of all the horror stories of our youth that everyone has to varying degrees, instead of using them as excuses for bad behaviour. I think you can be a little more creative rather than whining about your childhood, especially when there are such upstanding citizens who've suffered horrors we'll never know, like having to eat all their beans. Not naming any names.

I think some parents take some sadistic pleasure out of making their kids gag on vegetables to make up for their own childhood trauma. I remember being forced to finish my beans if I wanted to go back to the living room before the Polkaroo made an appearance and basically projectile vomited as a result. I'd do the same thing today, and not just for the Polkaroo. I think canned beans are one of the sickest jokes in world history. They actually should have had their own chapter. I eventually grew up to enjoy all foods, but if you ever try to serve me beans from a can, somebody is going to get hurt. Those cans are heavy before they're opened and I've got a good arm. Fair warning.

chapter 25:
keeping a journal

The importance of keeping a journal of your life experiences cannot be overstated. Each day is made up of so many learning opportunities, some large, some small, that we cannot possibly retain them all for reflection in the future without some sort of record. Often, we don't even realize something was noteworthy until we pause at the end of the day to think about anything noteworthy to write about. I hope you're taking notes.

When enough years go by, reading past journal entries can be just like reading another person's writing and thoughts, and you become your own teacher, your own friend, and your own inspiration. Sometimes I throw my head back in laughter and say out loud "Oh that David, what a character! I can't wait to see what happens to him tomorrow. I'm sure it'll be a disaster." Bystanders think I'm reading an engaging novel, but no, it's just my own enthralling, unpublished memoir. Feel free to read it after I'm dead.

Though some pages from long ago can be painful to read, it's interesting to see how we responded to life's trials back then and compare that to how we would handle them now that we're older and wiser. Or at least older. I find that I handle most things more slowly now and with more joint pain.

Sometimes finding things to write about can be a real challenge when you've had one of those days where pretty much all you did was exist, and probably didn't even do that very well either. This is when you get to exercise some creativity and look at your stagnant day from different angles. Start rambling about what you might do to make tomorrow better and go from there. There are a limited number of things we can say about today, while tomorrow has limitless possibilities, unless you die. In that case, you won't have to write in your journal anyway so who cares. It's too bad though really since that would make a pretty interesting entry.

One thing I love about reflecting on past journal entries is being reminded that whatever bad feelings I might have about my current situation, I have felt before. Though it is very often for different reasons, the underlying emotions and feelings that result are identical, and since I got through it before, I know I will again. This is especially true of heartbreak, and I don't mean only the romantic kind. No amount of therapy sessions, self-help books, or wine can make up for reading that one letter to yourself about how you've survived before. I think tonight I'll write about how this chapter ended up really serious and boring and how discouraged it made me feel, so that when I'm writing another book years from now, I'll remember I survived that too.

chapter 26:
gravity

A woman named Edith once worked in a dental office where she prided herself on her organizational skills, which included a vast and elaborate filing system kept in an array of very old and heavy metal filing cabinets placed against a wall where the floor had kind of a slant to it.

One day, as she went to search for a file in the bottom drawer, the top drawer rolled out and the whole thing fell over and landed on her. She didn't have a will made up because she never thought something like that would ever happen to her, so her kids started fighting over her furniture and fine china and whatever and ended up never speaking again.

chapter 27:
small talk

We've all been there, whether it be in a car, an elevator, or with a bad date at a banquet who left us standing alone at the dessert table and forced to mingle with their coworkers when we didn't even want to be there in the first place. I'm referring, of course, to small talk.

Small talk is like the filler they stuff hot dogs with. Nobody's really sure what part of the pig it is and nobody cares either, but they have to fill it with something or else it would just be a flimsy piece of intestinal skin in a bun and who wants to eat that? What most people don't realize is that the entire conundrum could be avoided by just not having a hot dog. They're just empty calories that make your head fat. This is still a metaphor, just in case I lost you already.

I'm not sure at what point in human evolution we developed a fear of awkward silences, but it has resulted in some rather unfortunate conversations in my lifetime, I'll tell you that right now. I really don't know why we need to fill a quiet moment with meaningless banter when we don't even have anything worthwhile to discuss or communicate. Now somebody's going to say it's to foster relationships and make friends, but I would submit that small talk is just as responsible for preventing them too. How many times were you interested in getting to know somebody until they said something?

Let's take a look at an example of small talk from my own personal experience in the waiting area of a mechanic's garage the other day. Nothing like being accosted by a complete stranger with superfluous blather while waiting for bad news and a humungous repair bill:

Figure 27.1 - Small talk

Sooo...
What do you think
of this weather
we're having?

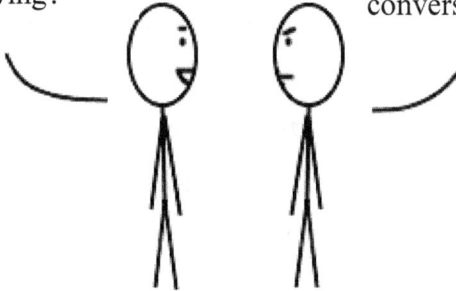

Who gives a crap?
It's bleak and dreary.
Just like this
conversation.

Another gentleman also tried to engage me in a discussion about international politics and was a real doomsayer. Obviously, I was having no part of his fear mongering. If it's necessary for me to partake in these conversations with strangers it better at least be on a topic that is positive and uplifting that I can relate to. Imagine someone trying to bring me down with their negativity!

The best way out of these precarious situations is to simply nod and offer the occasional "mmhmm" and "I know, eh?" until they eventually tire and move on like a predator on Animal Planet who stalks a pray for an hour to no avail and finally realizes they should look elsewhere before they starve.

Waiting rooms often have a television in the corner with some insanely boring programming on that you can stare at long enough to give the impression you're far too engrossed in it to engage. This only causes problems when it's something like the news that generates more unsolicited talking points.

Another technique that has worked for me, especially in Canada, is to agree with them about how cold the weather is and put my earmuffs back on and then keep saying "Pardon?" They're the ones who brought it up after all. I got some puzzled looks when I tried this in the summer but it was no less effective, especially while I was waiting to see my therapist. Yeah that's right, I sometimes need help too. Surprise!

chapter 28:
the art of conflict

I know a lot of you would rather not face it, but conflicts can and will arise. You should think of arguments like a game, and if someone in your life is going to force you to play, you might as well play to win.

You might think the key to having an edge in any conflict is being right, but that couldn't be further from the truth. There are so many different aspects to getting the upper hand in a conflict that people throughout the ages have truly raised it to the level of an art form. That is why court cases become such a spectacle and guilty parties end up getting off scot-free and released back into society thanks to lawyers who probably read this chapter. You're welcome.

So if the facts are not in our favour, what can we do to come out victorious in a conflict? I'm going to show you some exercises you can do in front of the mirror to sharpen your skills.

Let's start by realizing that most conflicts revolve almost entirely around our speech, and that *how* we say something is just as important as *what* we are saying. Below is an example sentence we can work with to examine how putting emphasis on different words can create an entirely different outcome.

"Excuse me, sir, but I was sitting here first."

This is a typical scenario. You come back to your chair to find somebody else is sitting in it. Let's see how different variations of the sentence help us to be victorious in this conflict:

Variation #1: "Excuse me, sir, but I was sitting here FIRST." This is a classic opener. Emphasis on "first". A good one for beginners as it relies on stating the obvious. I was here first, you were here second. Relinquish control of the chair to its rightful occupant.

Variation #2: "EXCUSE ME, sir, but I was sitting here first."
Emphasis on "excuse me" makes it appear that you are so completely appalled and in utter shock that somebody could be rude enough to steal your chair that it takes any respectable person by surprise and makes them instinctively apologetic.

Variation #3: "Excuse me, sir, but I was SITTING here first."
I have no idea what you're doing on that chair but it obviously isn't for its intended purpose, you weirdo. Causes self-doubt and insecurity.

Variation #4: "Excuse me, SIR, but I was sitting here first."
Emphasis on "sir" implies she is a man, immediately throwing her off and giving you the advantage.

Variation #5: "EXCUSE ME SIR BUT I WAS SITTING HERE FIRST!"
Pure, unadulterated rage. You better just get off the damn chair. Now.

I hope you can see all the different approaches you can take now to the same argument depending on the circumstances. Try practicing on your spouse tonight and let me know how it goes.

chapter 29: water

Apparently, a large percentage of our body is actually just water, and we're all basically a bunch of walking, talking, bloated water balloons inhabiting this planet, though I know some people who are definitely full of something else.

This probably explains why humans are so drawn to water. We drink it, swim in it, wash with it, and pay exorbitant amounts of money to have a view of it wherever we are. The sounds of rainfall or a running stream are among the most soothing the earth has to offer as far as relaxation and meditation go. If you've never been to Niagara Falls, I highly recommend it. You aren't going to find a better place to take a nap, or ride in a barrel, or both.

Water also provides a safer mode of transportation between continents on luxury ships. When planning my vacation, I often find that I am asking myself if I would rather drown, or scream and plummet for 30,000 feet and *then* drown. It always ends up being a no-brainer to me. If your boat hits an iceberg at least there's a chance you might be rescued. I'm pretty sure nobody's going to pull up alongside and give you a ride while you're hurtling towards the earth from above the clouds. Just something to think about.

Swimming is great exercise, whether just in your leisure time, or waiting to be rescued, but I prefer to stick to bodies of fresh water only, because the kinds of monsters that lurk in the murky ocean water don't really do it for me. I'm always amazed by people who casually breaststroke atop the ocean waves with full knowledge that at any random moment a set of extraterrestrial looking jaws could breach the surface and bite them in half. I'm learning that people just like to play the odds with this sort of thing and don't ever really believe they're the ones holding the winning ticket for the next deadly Powerball, so to speak.

Not that fresh water lakes don't have their own dangers. I read in the news recently about a certain brain-eating amoeba that likes to hang out in the warm and shallow areas. Any activity that causes water to shoot up your nose puts you at risk, and I'm not sure what you can do in a lake that doesn't involve that. The last thing you want is this vicious lifeform parading around in your head and feeding on your brain like a zombie. There isn't exactly a lot you can afford to lose up there. I would imagine some amoeba end up pretty disappointed with the menu after all that work making it up someone's nose.

Most experts agree that people should drink anywhere between 8 and 300 glasses of water per day to promote healthy skin and make that disgusting sloshing sound in your belly when you're moving around on the couch. Who cares if your skin looks good when you have a date over and you sound like a walking aquarium on a stormy boat ride and have to pee every five minutes? Besides, water is the main ingredient in most beverages, including wine, so there are alternative ways to meeting this dietary requirement.

Most of my best memories in life have involved being either on or by the water, including kayaking on secluded lakes in Canada or vacationing in the tropics where the water is a breathtaking turquoise hue. As the earth becomes scorched by climate change and droughts become increasingly common, I know that when it is all gone, I will miss it...

I will miss it.

chapter 30:
red wine

"Do not look on the wine when it is red,
When it sparkles in the cup,
When it goes down smoothly;
At the last it bites like a serpent and stings like a viper."
Proverbs 23:31-32

I propose a toast, since we're nearing the end of our time together, and what better topic to celebrate with than the romantic and ancient allure of red wine. Some people think that wine is an acquired taste, but if you ask me, so is their company.

The Bible includes many warnings about the consumption of wine and other alcohol, but allows for it also in moderation like most things. There is nothing like sharing a bottle of good wine with a friend and some stimulating conversation, and by sharing a bottle, I mostly mean that we'd each have our own and would be sharing the experience. Sharing one bottle would be like taking a little bite out of a cupcake and passing it back and forth for a few seconds till it's gone and you're both sitting there staring at each other like "Wow, I wish I could have eaten the whole thing. Who shares a cupcake? There isn't even enough for one person, much less two. Even if there were lots of cupcakes, you wouldn't both eat the same one! IT'S LUNACY!" It's what I'd be thinking anyway. So get your own damn cupcake.

If you're wondering why I've singled out red over white in this chapter, it's not that I don't enjoy a cold glass of pinot grigio on a hot summer day, but there's something about the warm heaviness of red that is more conducive to my vampire-like persona. I love that first sip of merlot when it's been quite a while since my last glass, so every so often I'll go a few hours without having one. Friends often tease me about how much wine I drink, but I also tease them about how I have to drink in order to be around them and find them interesting, and that's the sort of back and forth, good-natured ribbing that friendships are made of.

The trick is to be cautious and extremely aware of that thin line that has intrigue, invigoration, and sensitivity on one side, and debauchery, humiliation and hostility when crossed.

Indeed, a red wine-stained tongue can become quite venomous. Or so I've heard.

I probably should have suggested opening a bottle at the outset of this book instead of waiting till the end. Maybe you would have been a little more receptive to my ideas and felt inspired. Wine has a tendency to heighten the senses and make music and art even more beautiful and dreams seem just a little more within reach.

On the other hand, you might have gotten a little bit lippy with me and kept trying to interject your own "ideas", and then we'd have had a problem. A good precaution for this I've found over the years when having friends over for a drink is to incorporate the use of a talking stick. If you're not familiar with the concept, you basically pass around a large wooden stick and only the person holding it is allowed to speak. You can either pass it to the next person when you're finished, or bludgeon them with it if they speak out of turn. I've been able to convince most guests that the red stains on the end of mine are just from spilled red wine at past events so that they're not overly fearful of the idea at the beginning.

It's also interesting how different beverages have their different acceptable glasses. You don't drink coffee out of a beer stein (except at the start of a work week), you don't drink rum out of a champagne flute (except at weddings), and you certainly don't drink wine out of anything but a wine glass. It just tastes different and feels awkward. Please don't serve me wine in one of those "stemless" wine glasses either. I'm not that worldly. And that's not a stemless wine glass FYI, it's just a glass. Otherwise a coffee mug is also a stemless wine glass with a handle. Maybe I'll just start serving it in a barrel or a dog dish then and you can lap it up on all fours and I can start a new trend that makes me feel cool and contemporary just like stemless wine glass users.

In contrast to adding a little passion to some otherwise dry conversation, wine also can have a calming effect at the end of a stressful day. I'm pretty sure I've earned my glass after spending all this time trying to give advice and help people, so let's open another bottle and wrap this up so we can both get on with our lives. Time is in short supply, as we will now examine in the next, and final chapter.

chapter 31:
Death.

Y ou will note that this is the only chapter heading in which I utilize proper capitalization and punctuation, and that is out of respect for the finality of it all. I rarely use the word without a full stop, even when I say it mid-sentence, but I'll attempt to refrain from that habit temporarily for the sake of lucidity.

One of the most fascinating aspects of humanity is the absolute certainty that all lives will expire at one point or another, and yet we only seem to fear death and think about it when we believe it is near. We all just go about our business every day, working, playing, and dreaming, in complete ignorance of the fact that tomorrow may never come.

I suppose it has to be this way or everyone would just be running around with their arms flailing in the air screaming "THE END IS NIGH!" and that would get old for people pretty fast. I know from experience. It's just strange to me that it's exactly what happens during a disaster even though the only difference is that death is approaching faster than we thought it would. Why do people scream and cry when they're being chased by an axe murderer but don't scream and cry while they're having their Sunday morning coffee even though death is still approaching with the same degree of certainty but just at a slower pace?

Most people agree that we cannot go through life in fear of death, but I maintain that thoughts of impending death can actually be a very powerful tool to mitigate fear and stress about things in this life that have no bearing whatsoever on our final destination. For example, instead of stressing about that important meeting coming up in your job, or that failure to complete a certain task to someone else's standards, we might put those worries and frustrations in perspective by remembering that some day, not only will we be dead, but everyone who put expectations on us will be dead too. And probably before us *high five*.

The truth is that almost everything that people worry and stress about in a day has no eternal value or importance whatsoever and won't matter after you're gone. So with that in mind, here is my final bit of advice for you:

Make sure to let go of any concerns that are of this world and have no connection to your soul and your belief about where your soul is going after your impending death. We are not taking anything with us from this world into the next except for those beliefs, so question the motivation behind everything you do, and everything you say, and weigh it against what will matter after you are gone, because each year flies by faster than the one before it. "You are just a vapour that appears for a little while and then vanishes away." (James 4:14). Or as my 7th grade bus driver put it one stormy morning as we all sat nervously watching her try to navigate through the violent winds and torrential rain: "This little bus is gonna get blown off the highway like a fart in the mist!"

How do you like that? Finally some serious advice. I always wanted to write a book with a twist ending. I am totally like the M. Night Shyamalan of self-help authors. I bet you didn't see that one coming. Unless of course you're one of those people who reads the last page of a book first. If that's the case, you deserved to have the ending ruined for you, as well as everything else bad that happens to you today, including death.

♫ *ding DING dong* ♫ This concludes our broadcast day. Please rise for the national anthem.

For more by David Russell Bordowitz

please visit:

www.LetterToTheWorld.com

www.ingramcontent.com/pod-product-compliance
Lightning Source LLC
Chambersburg PA
CBHW061727020426
42331CB00006B/1124